LIVING WITH LOSS, HEALING WITH HOPE

Also by Earl A. Grollman

Bereaved Children and Teens: A Support Guide for Parents and Professionals (editor)
Caring and Coping When Your Loved One Is Seriously Ill
Concerning Death: A Practical Guide for the Living (editor)
Explaining Divorce to Children (editor)
In Sickness and in Health: How to Cope When Your Loved One Is Ill
Judaism in Sigmund Freud's World
Living When a Loved One Has Died
Living When a Young Friend Commits Suicide: Or Even Starts Talking about It (with Max Malikow)
Rabbinical Counseling (editor)
Straight Talk about Death for Teenagers: How to Cope with Losing Someone You Love
Suicide: Prevention, Intervention, Postvention
Talking about Death: A Dialogue between Parent and Child
Talking about Divorce and Separation: A Dialogue between Parent and Child
The Working Parent Dilemma (with Gerri L. Sweder)
Time Remembered: A Journal for Survivors
What Helped Me When My Loved One Died
When Someone You Love Has Alzheimer's: The Caregiver's Journey (with Kenneth S. Kosik, M.D.)
When Your Loved One Is Dying
Your Aging Parents: Reflections for Caregivers (with Sharon Grollman)

Living with Loss, Healing with Hope

A JEWISH PERSPECTIVE

Rabbi Earl A. Grollman

Beacon Press
Boston

Beacon Press
25 Beacon Street
Boston, Massachusetts 02108-2892
www.beacon.org

Beacon Press books
are published under the auspices of
the Unitarian Universalist Association of Congregations.

17 16 15 14   12 11 10 9

This book is printed on acid-free paper that meets the uncoated
paper ANSI/NISO specifications for permanence as revised in 1992.

Text design by Preston Thomas
Composition by Wilsted & Taylor Publishing Services

Library of Congress Cataloging-in-Publication Data
Grollman, Earl A.
Living with loss, healing with hope : a Jewish perspective / Earl A. Grollman.
p.   cm.
ISBN 978-0-8070-2813-1 (paperback)
1. Death—Religious aspects—Judaism.   2. Bereavement—Religious aspects—
Judaism.   3. Bereavement—Psychological aspects.   4. Jewish mourning
customs.   5. Consolation (Judaism).   I. Title.
BM634.4.G76 2000
296.4'45—dc21   00-008484

To all the mourners
who have taught me
not only about death
but about
the meaning of life

Comfort, oh comfort my people. —*Isaiah 40:1*

CONTENTS

INTRODUCTION

Death doesn't just happen
to the person who dies.
It also happens
to those left behind.

This book is about
the anguish of losing a loved one,
whether it is
    a spouse, a parent,
    a sibling, a child,
    a dear friend.

This book is also about life,
healing,
and finding a way
through your grief.

The rites of Jewish mourning unite two basic themes:
    Kevod ha-met, respect for the person who died, and
    Kevod ha-chai, respect for those who survive.

These rites helped to guide and support
generations of Jews
in their journey through sorrow.

It is my hope and prayer
that this book may
bring you a measure of solace and strength
as you journey
"through the valley of the shadow of death."

Zichrono/Zichronah li-veracha.
May his/her memory be for a blessing.

Grief

Grandfather, you were the pillar of fire in front of the camp,
and now we are left in the camp alone, in the dark;
and we are so cold and so sad.

> —Noa Ben-Artzi Philosof, age seventeen, spoken at the funeral of
> her grandfather, Israeli prime minister Yitzhak Rabin

The funeral is over.
The rabbi has said the traditional prayers.

So many people have come
to the *Shiva*, the house of mourning,
to offer their condolences.

But now you are alone,
  really alone.

Your loved one *is* dead.

The life
you shaped together
no longer exists.

Death has struck
like a cyclone.

Your life is shattered, uprooted.

You stand apart
in a devastated landscape.

I am racked with grief;
Sustain me in accordance with Your word.
—Psalm 119:28

Who knew that
grief would hurt so much?

*Since my husband's death,
I feel as though I've fallen
into a dark pit, separate
from everyone and everything.*
    —A widow

Give voice to the anguish
in your heart.

Talk.
Weep.
Rage.

You grieve deeply
because you loved deeply.

Grief is love not wanting to let go.

Don't compare your loss
with the loss of others.

Each death is different.
Each bereavement is unique.

When it is the death of a child,
it is the death of your future.

When it is the death of a parent,
it is the death of your past.

When it is the death of a spouse,
it is the death of the present.

Your grief is your own.

No one can know how you feel.
No one can shoulder the pain for you.

But there can be solace in the presence of others—
  people who love you and want to help,
  people who also mourn the loss of your beloved.

And there can be solace in the rich sources
of our Jewish faith.

That is why, during the *Shiva*,
friends and family
come together
    to offer condolences,
    to offer help,
    to recall the life they shared with your loved one.

Comforting the mourner is an act
of loving kindness toward both
the living and the dead.
          —Kitzur Shulkhan Arukh 193:11

Sometimes in their attempt to console,
people may say things
that are so insensitive.

Try to understand.

Most of us feel awkward
and ignorant
when faced with
death.

We really don't know what to say
or do.

Before the tragedy in your life,
you might have made the same kind of remark.

When my child was killed in an accident
And people said that it was God's will,
I wanted to scream.
            —A bereaved mother

Try to draw comfort
from the sound of friends' voices,
    if not from their words,

from the closeness of their bodies
standing near you,
    even though you feel so alone.

Try to draw solace
from the knowledge of their love
    and concern
    and sympathy.

Perhaps they too may have lost
    a brother, a sister,
    a father, a mother,
    a son, a daughter,
    or a friend.

A Chasidic commentary
explains why yod yod *is a name for God:*

When one yod *(Jew) is close to another* yod—
when one Jew gives another a hand
in loving support—

God's presence is with them.

The Many Faces of Mourning

My God, my God,
Why have you forsaken me?
I call by day,
But you do not answer,
And by night,
But find no rest.

   —Psalm 22

Loss is the nonnegotiable side of life.

So much of the meaning of your future existence
is determined by how you cope
with your loved one's death.

When a loved one dies,
there is no way to predict
how you will feel.

You may cry hysterically,
or feel hollow
and numb.

You may lash out in anger
against family and friends,
or you may cling to them
as a mooring in a storm.

You may question whether
you will ever smile
or trust the world again.

*When my sister died, I thought
there was something wrong with me
when I lost control of my emotions.*
      —A bereaved brother

Just as no love is the same,
so no loss is the same.

Each person experiences grief in his or her
own way.
There is no right or wrong way to grieve.

Grief is like a circular staircase.
It manifests itself in different ways.

You may be calm one moment—
in turmoil the next.

Shock
Denial
Panic
Anger
Guilt
Physical distress
Depression

These reactions aren't neat sequential steps or stages leading you through the maze of grief.

Like a roller coaster, they are recurring themes of anguish in confronting a devastating loss.

Learning about the emotions of grief
may help you understand
your own barrage of feelings.

Just remember:
  Grief takes time
  and courage
  and patience.

Try your best to be loving
with yourself.

Since there is no set timetable
for bereavement,
each one must find his or her own path
to acceptance and healing.

Take as long as you need.

All garments must be rent
opposite the heart . . .
for the mourner has to
expose the heart.
　　　　—Kitzur Shulkhan Arukh 195:3–4

Shock

You may be numb.

You may feel like a victim
of a violent windstorm—
swept away by forces
you didn't expect and
can't control.

Nothing seems real.

You're not ready for this.

When I heard my friend was murdered,
my lips moved but no sound came out.
　　　—Member of a Jewish bereavement group

You stop listening, stop hearing.
You feel as if you have stopped breathing.

The initial shock of tragedy is wrapped
in an eerie, heavy silence.

Denial

"I don't believe it. It can't be true."
"How could this happen to my loved one?"
"How could this happen to me?"
"It must be a horrible mistake, a nightmare."

Denial is a coping mechanism,
a part of grief.

When life seems unbearable,
denial intervenes
and allows a temporary breathing spell.

Denial temporarily shields you
from facing
the enormity of the pain.

It lends you a cushion of time
before the reality of loss
crashes in upon you,
and you are swept into
the undertow of despair.

Neither the sun nor death
can be looked at
with a steady eye.
            —La Rochefoucauld

Panic

You feel like you are losing control.
Helpless, disoriented.

Your heart races.
You feel faint, nauseous.

"What will become of me?"
"If only I could disappear or run away."
"If only there were a forgetting pill."

After my child's death,
I found a quick escape through drinking and pills.
After a period of time, I was worse off than before.
I had to learn the hard way that
alcohol + drugs + grief = greater grief.
     —A bereaved father

You are in a fragile state.
Death has dealt you an awful blow.

You need time
to collect yourself
and draw on your inner resources.

There are no shortcuts through
the pain of bereavement.

Work your way through,
    moment by moment,
    hour by hour,
    day by day.

Anger

You may be angry at those around you.
Your nerves are raw.

You may want to strike out against those
who say the wrong things.

You may be short-tempered with friends
who avoid you as though
your collision with death were contagious.

You may be furious with family members
who are so involved with themselves
that they don't seem to care about you.

You may be enraged at the medical establishment
   for failing to save your loved one.

You may be angry with your loved one
   for abandoning you
   and plunging you into this hell.

You may be annoyed at yourself
   for feeling this overwhelming rage
   and resentment.

You may be furious with God
   for allowing this to happen.

I don't deserve this!
   —A frequent remark at support groups

Anger is not shameful or wrong.

It helps to release your anguish and frustration
at an intolerable situation.

Anger is a normal feeling,
a part of grief.

It can serve as a protective defense,
an alternative to feeling vulnerable and terrified.

With time, your anger may diminish.

Find ways to let it go.

- ☐ Consider a long walk.
- ☐ Work out at the gym.
- ☐ Scream out loud in a private place, for example, in your car or in the shower.
- ☐ Beat on a pillow with a tennis racket.
- ☐ Listen to music.
- ☐ Meditate.

Do whatever brings relief.

Long ago, I conquered my anger and placed it in my pocket.
I take it out when I need it.
        —Pinchas of Koretz

Guilt

Guilt may eat away at your insides.

You writhe with shame as you recall
  words of scorn and impatience,
  acts of exasperation and anger.

Why didn't you show your love more truly?
Why did you let trivial annoyances mar your enjoyment
  of your loved one's companionship?

When death comes, life is reexamined.
You become acutely aware of your failures,
   real or imagined.

You wish you could make amends
   for all the wrongs you committed,
   all the things you should have said and done.

If only . . . I had known she was suicidal.
   —A bereaved grandparent

What is past is past.
It cannot be changed.

All of us let loving feelings go unexpressed.
All of us fail people who care about us.

Accept your fallibility.
Blaming yourself will not bring your loved one
    back to life.

All you can do is to avoid in the future
    what you regret in the past.

Judaism teaches that God forgives.

Now you must learn how to forgive yourself.

Physical Distress

An aching heart
takes a physical toll on the rest of your body.

You may experience a variety of symptoms:
  stomachaches
  headaches
  strange rashes
  palpitations or dizziness
  tightness in your throat

Perhaps you fall in bed exhausted,
    then find that you cannot sleep.
Perhaps you sleep more than ever,
    but are still tired when you wake.

It hurts to breathe,
    . . . to move . . . to live.

I am weary with my groaning,
And I find no rest.
          —Jeremiah 45:3

Your body is responding to bereavement.
These ailments are real, not imaginary.

Stress weakens resistance to disease,
aggravating former medical conditions
and creating new problems.

Consult an understanding physician.
Eat a balanced diet.
Get some exercise.
Try your best to take good care of yourself.

Remember:
Neglecting your health
does not honor the memory of your loved one.

*I felt completely
drained after my father's death.*
        —A bereaved adult son

Depression

"Nothing matters anymore."
"Why go on?"

You feel drained, emotionally depleted.
In the world of grief, each of us is alone.

Maybe you can't stop crying.
Maybe you can't cry at all.
The slightest effort leaves you exhausted.

You may do strange things
   like getting lost on familiar streets,
   hearing the voice of your loved one,
   constantly daydreaming about the way things
      used to be,
   even forgetting your own name.

No, you are not crazy.

Depression is part of mourning
someone you love.

Like shock and denial,
depression is a way of shutting down the emotional
    system
in response to overload.

Depression is part of saying good-bye
to someone you care so much about.

Life doesn't seem worth living anymore.
—A bereaved mother

Depression is also the term used to describe
a serious medical condition.

How do you know if your depression is
a normal, appropriate grief response,
or if it has escalated into a clinical psychological concern?

The distinction is mainly a matter of degree:
    how long the depression lasts and
    how intense it is.

After a period of time, ask yourself,
"Am I stuck in my grief?"
"Can I find comfort in the support of friends?"
"Can I occasionally enjoy the things that used to bring
    me pleasure?"

If you have concerns about your mental well-being
or the length and depth of your depression,
don't hesitate to confer with your rabbi
or seek professional advice from a counselor or
    physician.

To acknowledge problems and seek help
are the most courageous
and responsible acts you can take.

Because I remember, I despair.
Because I remember, I have the right to reject despair.
    —Elie Wiesel

Healing and Recovering

Life and death
are brothers/sisters who dwell together.
They cling to each other
and cannot be separated.
—Bahya Ibn Pakuda, *Duties of the Heart*

Accepting Your Pain

"Why?"
"Why me?"
"Why did my loved one have to die?"

There are questions that have no answers.

Unanswered *whys* are part of life.

You cannot heal what you don't
allow yourself to feel.

Even though it may be the most difficult thing
you have ever done,

you must face reality.

You must acknowledge the pain
and attempt to live with it.

The Seal of God is Truth.
—*Talmud*

Expressing Your Feelings

Respect your feelings.

Sorrow, like the river, must be given vent
lest it erode its bank.

Allow yourself to mourn and grieve
for what was and
what could have been.

*Lament the dead [in] words
which break the heart. . . .*
        —Shulkhan Arukh: Yoreh Deah 344:1

Tears

Crying is one means of working your way
out of despair.

Crying is an honest expression of a grief
that transcends words.

When Sarah, our aged matriarch, died,
Her husband, Abraham,
"came to mourn and weep for her." (Genesis 23:2)

Tears strengthen me.
        —Morrie Schwartz, in a conversation with Ted Koppel

When members of a family,
both male and female,
adults and children,
cry together,
they share the
inexpressible pain of separation.

Of course, your weeping will not
bring back your loved one.
But that is why you cry.

Because you cannot bring your
beloved back to life.

When my wife died, I wanted to be strong, so I hid my emotions.
From childhood I was taught that "big boys don't cry."
Later on, I hit bottom because I was afraid to show my feelings.
   —*A widower*

Talking

In times of crisis,
silence is not golden.

Talk things out,
with friends, family, counselors, your rabbi.

You may need to repeat
over and over
all the circumstances surrounding your loss.

Call your feelings by their rightful names.
   "I am *angry.*"
   "I am *hurt.*"
   "I am *scared.*"
   "I am *sad.*"

Recount the good times you shared:
"Do you remember when . . . ?"

But don't be afraid to recall some of the difficult
    moments.
You can talk of those as well.
Death should not transform your loved one into a saint,
or the past into a paradise.
Each relationship is tinged with unhappiness
as well as joy.

That's life.

My heart moans within me!
I cannot hold my peace!
    —Jeremiah 4:19

Writing a journal is another way
to express inner thoughts and feelings.

You might start with
   "When I now hear your name mentioned, I . . ."
   "Since your death, my life . . ."
   "I miss . . ."
   "If only . . ."

You can say anything you wish
without being judged, criticized, or pitied.

Write about whatever eases your heart, mind, and soul:
   regrets, troubling fears, goals—both small and large—
   observations, wishes, dreams.
   Write letters or poems to yourself or to your loved one.

As you write, you unlock your feelings
and explore new dimensions of thoughts.
You delve deeper into the layers
of your convictions and doubts,
bringing welcome clarity and release.

What about the Children?

One person's death touches the lives of many.

Your children may have lost a parent, a sibling,
a grandparent,
or a treasured friend.

In the midst of your grief,
it is important that you reach out to them,
make time for them,
talk with them,
listen to them.

The world rests upon the breath
of the children in the schoolhouse.
—Shabbat, 119

Be truthful.

Do not conceal your own pain.
Give your children straightforward, honest explanations
in words that are appropriate to their age.
Encourage them to express their feelings.
Heed their actions as well as their words.

Help your children understand that it is
normal and healthy
to feel strong conflicting emotions.
It's also okay to feel a lack of emotion.

Denial, numbness, anger, tears, and despair
are natural reactions for children as well as adults.

A child can stand sorrow but not deceit.
        —*Rabbi Joshua Liebman, in* Peace of Mind

To be able to show grief openly
and to mourn without fear or embarrassment
helps both children and parents accept
the naturalness and pain of death.

Stay close to your children in this time of grief.
Hug them.
Comfort them.
Show them that your love for them is constant and
      strong,
and not lessened by the overwhelming sorrow you
      all feel.

Until my father told me how angry he felt
about my mother's death,
I thought he was mad at me.
      —A ten-year-old child

Death is bewildering.
It raises questions for which there are no easy answers.
   "Why did God let my sister die?"
   "What does it feel like to die?"
   "What happens to you when you are dead?"

Gently encourage your children
to ask whatever is on their minds.

Be honest about your own uncertainties.

You might say to your children,
"Lots of people think about death in different ways.

Tell me what you think."

As you strive to help your children,
you may discover explanations for yourself.

A philosopher said that learning from children
is the best opportunity
to assure a meaningful old age.

Community and Support

Rabbi Moshe Leib Sassover recounted a conversation he
   overheard between two villagers.

"Tell me, friend Ivan, do you love me?"
"I love you deeply."
"Do you know, my friend, what gives me pain?"
"How can I know that?"
"If you don't know what gives me pain, how can you say
   that you truly love me?"

Yes, the Sassover concluded, to love, truly to love, means
   to know what gives pain to your friend.

—Chasidic

We all need the support of others,
particularly when we are devastated
by agonizing loss.

A good friend can be a lifeline,
someone you can talk to honestly,
someone who will not judge you,
but accept you as you are.

Times of tragedy can be a crucible
in which friendships are tested.

You may feel abandoned by certain friends
who vanished even before the funeral,
or after a token condolence call.

Those friends may feel unequipped
to help you through your grief.
They may mistakenly think you want to be alone.
They, too, are frightened by death.

Try to forgive them.
After all, during these turbulent days,
there are many times
you don't understand yourself.

Remember that even the best of friends
cannot read your mind.
Communicate clearly.
If you repeatedly say, "I'm fine,"
how can your friends know
that you need their help?

Sometimes, a casual acquaintance
may step in to fill the breach,
help you through your despair,
and become a *new* true friend.

Who would believe that a person
I hardly knew
would be more helpful
than my family and friends?
            —A bereaved teenager

Many mourners find it helpful to
seek the company of others who have
experienced similar loss and sorrow.

A bereavement group can become a second family
during your journey of grief.

They understand when you ask,
"Why me?"

They understand when you say,
"I don't think I can make it."
"I don't think I want to live."

You learn together and lend each other support
as you begin the arduous task
of rebuilding your lives.

It's sometimes hard being with my old friends.
I feel I'm a burden to them, like I'm a fifth wheel.
But in my synagogue widow/widower group, I belong and
I am no longer alone.
     —*A widow/widower group member*

Solitude

In times of stress, you need time
to rest your body and your mind.
You need time to be alone.

Solitude is not loneliness.
Loneliness is the pain of being alone.
Solitude is satisfaction in being alive.

Solitude offers
   a sense of peace,
   a oneness with the natural world around you,
   a spiritual wholeness.

Go for a walk.
The rhythm of your step
releases the tension
in your body, mind, and spirit.

You become more aware
of yourself as a physical being,
a resilient, autonomous person moving through
          the world.

Spend some quiet time in a lovely, solitary place.
Let the sounds, sights, and smells of nature
surround and infuse you.

Three things conspire together in my eyes
To bring the remembrance of You ever before me:
The starry heavens,
The broad green earth,
The depths of my heart.
          —Solomon ibn Gabirol

Close your eyes, relax,
and listen to music.
Let the surge of sound
transport you to another world.

Consider prayer and meditation.

Seek healing solitude and peace
through whatever activity,
in whatever place,
feels best to you.

Reaching Out to Those in Need

You are not alone
in your journey through pain and crisis.

One touch of sorrow
makes the whole world kin.

Only a single person was created in the beginning,
to teach that if any individual causes a single person to perish,
Scripture considers it as though an entire world has been
          destroyed,
and if anyone saves a single person, Scripture considers it
as though a whole world had been saved.
          —Mishnah, Sanhedrin 4:5

Perhaps there is a cause or an organization
that was important to your loved one.
Reaching out can be a way to honor
the memory of your loved one
and continue his or her commitment.

Or consider going through the auspices
of your synagogue's social action committee
to volunteer at a hospital, a homeless shelter, a youth
    organization.

As you lift your hand
to lighten another's load,
you lighten your own as well.

It is plain that we exist . . . for those upon whose smiles and welfare our happiness depends, and for all those unknown to us personally but to whose destinies we are bound by the tie of sympathy.

　　　　—Albert Einstein

Spirituality

If you believe in God,
the death of your loved one
may leave you feeling betrayed or outraged.

God may appear distant and aloof,
too far away, too uninterested
to be of help.

"Why me, God? Why us?"

You may rage at God,
denouncing God for this unfair cruelty.

Your anger is a natural and normal response
to extreme anguish.
Questioning your faith is not an affront to God.
Doubts are part of the cycle of our religion.

Judaism allows your angry cry to heaven—
"How could you, God!"

What did I do unto You,
So that I am a burden to myself?
     —Job 7:20

Your anger at God
could be your form of prayer.
No one can hurt you like those closest to you,
those you trust the most.

To be furious at God could indicate
that God was once a presence in your life

and may be again.

Faith does not preclude grief.

Some people believe that
if you live a spiritual existence,
"goodness and mercy
will follow you all the days of your life."

Wrong!

Our Jewish faith is not an insurance policy
offering protection
against the cruel blows of fate.

God doesn't hand out prizes
based on how well you've lived.

Death is not a punishment
for your shortcomings or transgressions,
or for those of your loved one.

When they say, "It's God's will,"
I think God must be my enemy.
                    —A mourner

Death is an event that may shake the foundations
of the mourner's faith.

Yet faith also may have the power to sustain you
in the excruciating struggle
to accept the unacceptable.

"God, please help me through this ordeal."

As you face this struggle,
you may discover a measure of solace and peace,
a deeper insight into your faith,
as well as into your inner being.

No day without night and no night without day.
—Zohar I, 162a

One mourner said
that her spiritual anguish was so great
that she felt like Jacob
wrestling with the angel.

In the midst of her suffering
she found comfort in the presence of a power
greater than she.
No longer did she have to struggle alone
"in the valley of the shadows."

With both faith and doubts, she quoted Elie Wiesel:
    "God is the answers . . .
    and the questions too."

The Lord is my shepherd; I shall not want.
He maketh me to lie down in green pastures;
He leadeth me beside the still waters.
He restoreth my soul;
He guideth me in straight paths for His name's sake.
Yea, though I walk through the valley of the shadow of death,
I will fear no evil,
For Thou art with me;
Thy rod and Thy staff, they comfort me.
Thou preparest a table before me in the presence of mine enemies;
Thou hast anointed my head with oil; my cup runneth over.
Surely goodness and mercy shall follow me all the days of my life;
And I shall dwell in the house of the Lord forever.

    —Psalm 23

A New Life

To every thing there is a season, and a time
to every purpose under heaven:

A time to be born, and a time to die;
A time to plant, and a time to pluck up that which is planted;

A time to kill, and a time to heal;
A time to break down, and a time to build up;

A time to weep, and a time to laugh;
A time to mourn, and a time to dance.

—Ecclesiastes 3

Choosing Life

Grief ebbs, but it never ends.

The path you walk
is long and arduous.

Trust yourself and respect your feelings.
In time you will gradually
make peace with your loss.

Then, turn toward the future
with courage and resolve.

*I have set before you life and death, blessing and
curse. Therefore, choose life so that you and your
offspring may live.*
       —Deuteronomy 30:19

The Medicine of Time

An old saying tells us that "time heals."

In part, that is true.

With the passage of time,
the pangs of grief may become less sharp, less frequent.

But healing does not simply happen.
Healing is hard work.

You must help time to do its healing.

I feel worse today
than when my beloved died months ago.
—A mourner

Right after your loved one died, it may have been
    unbearable
to think about sorting through
photographs, letters, and personal mementos.

Those tangible reminders of your life together
may have been too painful to look at,
too painful to touch.

Maybe you were tempted to throw them away.

Aren't you glad you didn't do it?

Concrete mementos of the past
can help you cherish the memory of your loved one.

Photos and letters can help you tell others
of the life you shared
so that your loved one's story will live on
in the hearts and thoughts of friends and family,
and even in the memories of generations unborn.

Redemption lies in remembering.
—Ba'al Shem Tov
inscribed on the entrance to Yad Vashem in Jerusalem

One Day at a Time

Grief moves you to a new dimension,
a world apart from the bustle and concerns
of everyday life.

It's hard to reenter the mainstream
When you feel that you no longer belong.

Withdrawing into isolation is not the answer.

Slowly but steadily,
you must find a way
to reengage with the business of living.

It may be difficult to face other people,
especially those outside your immediate circle of friends.

Leaving your home for the first time
can be a frightening experience.

You may surprise yourself by weeping
when an acquaintance expresses sympathy.

But once you have done it,
it is over.

You need not go through the ordeal
with that person again.

You have begun to attend
to the task of shaping a new life for yourself.

Life is not like before.
Not like you would choose—

But you are choosing
to begin again.

All beginnings are difficult.
        —Talmud, Ta'anit 10B

You may be tempted to make a radical change in your
      life—
   to sell your house,
   to move someplace different,
   to make a fresh start,
away from your familiar home and all the painful
      memories.

Wait awhile.

The time is not right for major decisions.
Your judgment is still uncertain.
You are still in horrible pain.
Getting used to a new life takes time, thought, and
      patience.

"Yea, though I *walk* through the valley of the shadow of
      death . . ."
As the psalmist says, you must *walk* through grief.
You cannot *run* through it, or away from it.
Walk through it, slowly and gently.

Make a list of activities for the next days.
You don't have to follow it exactly,
but have a plan.

Be sure to schedule some diversions,
activities that will take you outside
the house.

Set aside time to immerse yourself
in physical or artistic pursuits such as
painting, gardening, music, or sport.

Plan opportunities to meet new people,
or spend time with dear friends,
doing activities you enjoy together.

Gradually, rediscover and reclaim aspects of yourself
that have been put on hold,
overshadowed by
the magnitude of your sorrow.

You honor your loved one
through this renewed commitment to life.

Every moment of life is a new arrival, a new beginning. Those who
say that we die every day, that every moment deprives us of a
portion of life, look at moments as time past. Looking at moments as
time present, every moment is a new arrival, a new beginning. . . .
—Rabbi Abraham Joshua Herschel

Significant Days

The road to recovery is not smooth.
You will experience setbacks.

Holidays, birthdays, anniversaries,
High Holydays, Passover, and other significant days
are often especially difficult.

One person compared the experience
to having a wound that is healing
be reinjured,
and begin to bleed again.

My son always sat between me and my father
at the Passover Seder—the three generations together.
But this year, I sat next to my father.
It was as if no chair or person ever existed.
Not one person mentioned my child's name.
Unbelievable—like he never lived!
            —A bereaved parent

You may be able to ease your grief
by planning how you might spend the day.

Think about what would be best for you.
You need to feel less like a victim,
    and more like a survivor.

It may help to change your usual rituals,
or start new traditions.

Choose those people with whom you are most
        comfortable,
with whom you can speak of your loved one,
with whom you can cry or even laugh at memories.

You might
   tell favorite stories,
   look through a photo album,
   light a memorial candle.

Going to the synogogue for services
or private prayer and meditation
may be inspirational and helpful.

If you are able, try to enjoy parts of the day,
even with the painful recollections
and awareness of loss.

God separated the light from
the darkness.
       —*Genesis 1:4*

Letting Go
. . . and Getting On with Life

Feeling better is not an indication that you loved less.
Rather it is a sign of your determination to let go
and get on with life
despite its bitterness and tribulations.

It means taking each day as it comes,
making the most of it,
resolving that you will survive
and celebrate your loved one's life.

When people ask, "When are you going to get over it?"
I want to shout, "I'll never get over it."
What I'm trying to do is get through it.
—A bereaved spouse

A basic tenet of Judaism
is to find purpose in *this* world.

Death marks the end of every life,
but it is not the meaning of life,
nor does it diminish the preciousness of a beloved life
      that was shared.

Life is for the living.

Now after the Yahrzeit, *as the scars begin to heal,*
I feel like a tree covering itself with new growth.
My loved one is dead. But I am alive.
It's time to start living again.
          —A widow

Growing through Grief

When someone you love dies,
you confront your own mortality.

How suddenly aware
you are
of the uncertainty and brevity of life.

For death
leads you to scrutinize your own beliefs—
deepening some convictions,
overturning others—
with a whole new set of priorities.

I have only one life and it's short enough;
why waste it on things I don't want most?
—Louis D. Brandeis

You may find yourself
drawn into the synagogue community,
deeply concerned with what it means to be a Jew
and to live Jewishly.

You may see this crossroads in your life
as an opportunity to become immersed
in the fundamentals of culture, ethics, and spirituality,
reclaiming your inner life,
caring for the soul as well as the world,
and finding a closer, more intimate
relationship with God.

The Eternal accepts every invitation.
You seek God? Extend an invitation.
    —*The Koretzer Rebbe (Chasidic)*

Death has led you to the edge of an abyss
of desolation.
It has threatened to overwhelm you with
despair and meaninglessness.

Now you must begin to build a bridge across the abyss
through those things that count the most—
  memory,
  family,
  friendship, and
  love.

Try to strike that delicate balance
between a yesterday that should
be remembered
and a tomorrow that must be created.

The memory of the
righteous shall be for
a blessing.
　　　—Proverbs 10:7

Shalom

In Hebrew it means
farewell,
peace,
welcome.

Shalom says *farewell* to the past.
At the funeral, and through the months of grieving,
you sorrowfully bid your loved one *shalom,* good-bye.

Shalom makes *peace* with what life has brought.
Through honoring your loved one's memory and
treasuring the life you shared together,
you strive to make peace with both life and death.

Shalom welcomes the future.
Your loved one has transformed and enriched your life.
Those gifts live on within you.
They give you strength and courage
as you walk forward to greet tomorrow.

Grief is a process.
Recovering is a choice.

Death is but a moment . . .
Love is forever.

Shalom.

For love is strong as death.
        —*Song of Songs*

A Ritual Guide for the Bereaved

The important thing is not how many
separate injunctions are obeyed,
but how and in what spirit we obey them.
　　　　—Baal Shem Tov

Thirty-five years ago, when I was immersed in research on loss and grief, I shared my findings with one of the most distinguished scholars in the field of thanatology. I will never forget his words: "Earl, I am not a member of your faith, but between you and me, if I wanted the soundest emotional and spiritual guidance to death, I would be a Jew."

Over the centuries the rabbis have created rituals that reflect not only their theological viewpoints but a profound understanding of the complex sociological and psychological aspects of the grief processes. Respect for the dead is delicately balanced with insights for the living.

Jewish rituals acknowledge the pain of grieving as they help mourners ease their way back to the rhythm of life. Through the observances of the funeral, interment, *Shiva, Sheloshim,* Unveiling, *Yizkor,* and *Yahrzeit,* the bereaved are afforded a sense of belonging, comfort, and hope. These symbolic customs are about change— remembrance, letting go, and moving on. In the face of death, Judaism offers the most potent remedies to strengthen the mind, body, and spirit.

Judaism is more than a creed; it is a way of life. And death is a reality of life. Just as there are diverse ways in which Jews throughout the ages have viewed life, so there are different approaches by which Jews practice the rites of death. Even though Judaism recognizes the value of continuity and tradition, there is no single path in regard to the rites of burial and manners of mourning. This chapter offers you a general overview of Jewish rituals; it is not intended as a comprehensive guide. For an understanding of the age-hallowed *Chevra Kadisha* (Burial Society), the hand-washing after interment, covering the mirrors, *Shiva* benches, tombstone inscription, and other mourning customs and traditions, the rabbi in your community would be your best companion in your pilgrimage through grief.

For the Jew, the ceremonies of death are of enormous significance. The Jewish religion offers rites that play a vital role in the healing work of grief. The bereaved must realize that a loved one is dead and that the void must be filled gradually in constructive ways. They should not suppress memories or the disturbing, even guilt-producing recollections that are an inevitable part of human relationships. Shock and grief are structured by defined solemn rites in which the entire family may participate. The family is supported by a community of faith in its readjustment to everyday living.

One becomes a mourner (*Avel* in Hebrew) upon the death of one of seven relatives: father, mother, husband, wife, son or daughter, brother or sister, including half brother or half sister.

From the moment that one learns of the death of a loved one, there are specific religious rites that help to order the mourner's life. A most striking expression of grief is the rending of the mourner's clothes (*Keriah*). In the Book of Genesis, when Jacob believed that his son Joseph was killed, the father "rent his garments" (37:34). Today many mourners indicate their anguish by cutting a black ribbon, usually at the funeral chapel or at the cemetery prior to interment. Some cut a portion of their clothes. The ceremony is performed standing up to teach the bereaved to "meet all sorrow standing upright."

THE FUNERAL

The Jewish funeral is a rite of separation. The presence of the casket actualizes the experience. Denial is transformed to the acceptance of reality. The public funeral affords the community an opportunity to offer support and share sorrow. All the emotional reactions that the bereaved are likely to experience—sorrow and loneliness, anger and rejection, guilt, anxiety about the future, and the conviction that nothing is certain or stable anymore—can be lessened by the support of caring friends.

Jewish rites and ceremonies help the bereaved to bear the painful loss. The rabbi recites those prayers that are expressive of both the spirit of Judaism and the memory of the deceased. The most commonly used, Psalm 23, expresses the faith of the members of the flock in the justice of the Divine Shepherd. From Psalm 144, "Lord, what is man?" comes the thought that our "days are as a shadow that passes away," but Psalm 90 counsels that there is immortality for those who have treasured their days with a "heart of wisdom." During the recitation of the prayer *El Molay Rachamim* ("God full of compassion"), the name of the deceased is mentioned. The eulogy of the dead (*Hesped*) is included in the service to recognize not only that a death has occurred but that a life has been lived.

The rabbis deem it a most worthy deed for the friends of the deceased not only to attend the funeral service but to follow the procession to the Jewish cemetery. The *Halva'yat Ha-mat* is the ultimate demonstration of honor and respect. At the graveside, the burial service is conducted. After the recitation of the Kaddish, the prayer of condolence is offered: *"Ha-makom Ye-nechem Etchem Bĕtoch She'ar Avelay Tziyon Vi Yerusha la'yim"* ("May the Eternal comfort you among the other mourners for Zion and Jerusalem"). By accepting death as a part of God's order for the world, Jews make death a part of life's plan. When death comes, one need not walk the lonely road alone.

AFTER THE FUNERAL

Shiva (meaning seven) refers to the first seven days of intensive mourning, beginning immediately after the funeral, with the day of burial counted as the first day. Mourning customs are not observed on Sabbaths or major Jewish Festivals, although these are counted toward the seven days.

Immediately upon returning from the cemetery, a light (*Shiva* candle) is lit and kept burning for the entire seven days. Proverbs (20:27) suggests "The spirit of humankind is the lamp of the Lord." One candle is sufficient for the entire household.

Throughout the *Shiva,* the bereaved remain at home receiving a continuous stream of condolence calls. Companionship lends the comfort of the loving concern of family and friends.

Even though children under the age of thirteen are exempt from many of the mourning rites, they should not be arbitrarily dismissed from the family gathering. They should be given the opportunity to face grief and mingle with their loved ones. Some children choose to share in the family duties such as answering the doorbell and telephone, and having their own friends visit with them.

Following the *Shiva* comes the *Sheloshim,* the thirty days. (The count of thirty includes the seven days of *Shiva.*) During this time mourners resume normal activity but avoid places of entertainment.

For a parent who has died, one recites Kaddish for eleven months beginning with the day of burial. The twelve-month mourning period is counted from the date of death. For others, *Sheloshim* concludes the period of bereavement.

Throughout the ritual mourning period, adults attend the *Minyan* (daily worship) as well as the Sabbath and Festival Services. They read aloud the Kaddish prayer, originally not a liturgy for the dead but a pledge from the living to dedicate one's life to the God of Life, "Magnified and Sanctified." When they say the Kaddish surrounded by other mourners, they join hands with others who have known anguish and death. This great sense of sorrow helps to unite human hearts through common sympathy and understanding.

The memorial prayer of *Yizkor* ("May God remember the soul of my revered") is said four times a year during the synagogue worship: *Yom Kippur, Shemini Atzeret* on *Sukkot, Pesach,* and *Shavuot.*

The anniversary of the death (*Yahrzeit*) is observed annually on the Hebrew date of death, commencing on the preceding day and concluding on the anniversary day at sunset. Kaddish is recited in the synagogue and the *Yahrzeit* candle is kindled.

The service commemorating the tombstone or plaque is called the Unveiling. The time of the Unveiling may be any time after *Sheloshim* and usually before the first year of mourning is over. Unveilings are not held on the Sabbath or Festivals. Any member of the family, a close friend, or, of course, a rabbi may intone the appropriate prayers, selected psalms, the *El Molay Rachamim,* and the Kaddish.

No one is the same after a bereavement. However, with time, mourners are expected to resume the normal activities of life. If the garment of the mourner was torn (*Keriah*), it can be mended and worn again. The scar is there, but life resumes its course. These rituals help the bereaved to acknowledge painful reality, honor the deceased, and begin to reaffirm life.

THEOLOGICAL CONCEPTS

In his book *The Jewish Mourner's Book of Why,* Rabbi Alfred Kolatch has correctly stated that it is impossible to integrate the diverse and distinct beliefs regarding an afterlife and label them Jewish. For example, in the beginning of the first Christian century, the Sadducees rejected a belief in an afterlife, while the Pharisees proclaimed that there *was* a world-to-come.

Many Jews derive comfort from a theological belief in the *Olam Haba,* "the World to Come," the traditional Jewish expression referring to the afterlife. The classical view articulated by the rabbis is that death is "a night between two days," a passage from one stage to another. "The rabbis," wrote Louis Ginzberg in *The Legend of the Jews,* "believed in another world and often spoke of rewards awaiting the righteous after their death." There was a belief in the existence of the soul after death. And for others there was a faith in *Techiyat ha-metim,* the reunion of the body and the soul standing together in judgment before God. In *The Death of Death,* Rabbi Neil Gillman affirms that "I recite the *Gevurot* benediction of the *Amidah* and praise the goodness and majesty of God who gives life to the dead."

A contemporary Orthodox thinker, the late renowned scholar Rabbi Joseph Soloveitchik, believed in directing our minds heavenward, but taking care not to be diverted from our primary task of establishing God's kingdom here upon earth. He expressed it this way: "The *Halachah* [Jewish law] is not at all concerned with a transcendent world. The World to Come is a tranquil, quiet world that is wholly good, wholly everlasting, and wholly eternal. However, . . . the task of the religious individual is bound up with the performance of commandments, and this performance is confined to this world, to physical, con-

crete reality, to clamorous, tumultuous life, pulsating
with exuberance and strength" (*Halak-hik Man*).

So again the question is raised: "Is Judaism a this-
worldly or other-worldly faith?" The answer is that it is
both. The paradox was so poignantly expressed in the
statement of the second-century teacher R. Jacob (*Avot*
4:17): "Better is one hour of repentance and good deeds in
this world than the whole life of the world to come; yet
better is an hour of blissfulness of spirit in the world-to-
come than the whole life of this world."

In the Jewish movements there may be a difference of
opinion. There are many thoughts, yet none is declared
authoritative and final. The tradition teaches, but at the
same time seems to say that there is much we do not know
and still more we have to learn. Even then, only God can
completely discern the mysteries of life and death.

TORAH AND STUDY

How does one learn about Jewish beliefs regarding an af-
terlife as well as about other sources of spirituality? Or as
Job said (28:12), "But wisdom, where shall it be found?
And where is the place of understanding?"

Check both the public and synagogue libraries. In re-
cent years a multitude of books have been written especially from spiritual, medical, and psychological perspec-
tives concerning the credibility of life after life. It has also
become very popular for rabbis from every branch of Judaism to share their views of the transcendent world.

But why confine yourself to a fractional aspect of Jewish thought? All rabbis have witnessed mourners attend-
ing a *Minyan* and then deciding while present in the synagogue to attend an adult study class. What a revelation!
Before their beliefs were predicated upon a juvenile Judaism, materials they learned in order to become a Bar or Bat

Mitzvah. Now they are able not only to study about their past but to gain fresh prescriptions of healing for the adult spirit and psyche.

It is important to start slowly, perhaps to attend an adult summer camp, to go to a retreat study center, or to join with a partner (*Chevrutah*) in a spiritual reawakening. "Therefore [teach them] one command and then another one, one line and then another, a little here, a little there" (Isaiah 28:10). Renewal is a task that is never completed.

HEALTH AND SPIRITUALITY

In the past, science separated health and spirituality. Spirituality was the province of clergy and theologians. Science focused upon the body's remarkable mechanisms with high-tech MRI scans and electron microscopes.

Physicians and psychotherapists are at last appreciating the mind-body connection. Clinical studies have demonstrated that when some patients incorporated a blend of faith, prayer, and worship in their medical treatment, they experienced enhanced physical and mental health. Prayer and meditation might slow the heart and breathing rate and diminish stress-related disorders. Attendance at worship could reduce hypertension and feelings of hostility, depression, and aloneness. Through spirituality, some may find a way to address and deal with grief and loss, and seek new meaning and purpose in life.

In Judaism, there has always been the recognition that humankind is more than a physical or biological unit, and that human health demands nourishment from a variety of deep inner resources. Jewish healing centers are burgeoning around the United States, Canada, and elsewhere, some as departments of Jewish Family Service Agencies and others as freestanding programs affiliated with other agencies or synagogues. These centers assist their clients in achieving a more fulfilling Jewish life experience, whatever problems they may be facing.

For many Jews, death has left them with an overpowering sense of agony, hurt, and isolation, an isolation that extends to God. They may be too devastated to pray. There is an expression: "When the mind is ready, the teacher appears." In time, these mourners may heed the words of the prophet: "When you call Me and come and pray to Me, I will hear you. When you seek Me, you will find Me. If you search for Me with all your heart, I shall let you find Me" (Jeremiah 29:12–14).

Prayer and meditation may provide needed opportunity for reflection and introspection, and may help mourners get in touch with their strength and faith and allow them at last to express their panic and fears and begin to transcend their despair. Meditation especially allows mourners to be with themselves in order to go beyond themselves. As they center and refocus, they may gain access to regions of their innermost selves.

THE COMMUNITY

Being embraced by a loving community is fundamental to Jewish spirituality. Grief, while being intensely personal, is also essentially social. The *Edah,* the community, is a primary component of healing and fellowship. Together, the community expresses its loss and hope through affirming words, observances, and prayers that have been uttered by Jews throughout the centuries. There is no sounder advice than that given in *The Ethics of the Fathers* (*Pirke Avot* 2:5): "Do not separate yourself from your community."

According to Jewish tradition, one of the community's highest commandments (*Mitzvah*) is *Nichum Avelim,* "comforting the mourner." So essential is this commandment that, according to Ecclesiastes 7:2 "It is better to go to the house of mourning, than to go to the house of feasting." For good reason, many synagogues, federations, and funeral homes have established support groups for the bereaved. Rabbi Daniel Roberts of Temple Emanu-El in Cleveland, Ohio, has pioneered this movement with his *Nechamah* (comfort team). Former mourners are trained to listen to and accompany those whose loved ones have recently died. They learn communication skills and an understanding of the stages and processes of grief. With sensitivity, compassion, and personal presence, these comforters aid magnificently in the painful struggle through bereavement. In the words of the prayer book: "Grief is a great teacher when it sends us back to serve and bless the living" (*Gates of Prayer*).